kid STARS!

Brenda Song

Katherine Rawson

PowerKiDS press
New York

Published in 2010 by The Rosen Publishing Group, Inc.
29 East 21st Street, New York, NY 10010

Copyright © 2010 by The Rosen Publishing Group, Inc.

All rights reserved. No part of this book may be reproduced in any form without permission in writing from the publisher, except by a reviewer.

First Edition

Editor: Nicole Pristash
Book Design: Kate Laczynski
Book Layout: Julio Gil
Photo Researcher: Jessica Gerweck

Photo Credits: Cover Alberto E. Rodriguez/Getty Images; p. 4 Jewel Samad/AFP/Getty Images; p. 7 © AP Photo/Mirek Towski/DMI via AP; pp. 8, 12 Kevin Winter/Getty Images for HRTS; p. 11 © 20th Century Fox/Zuma Press, Inc.; p. 15 Jesse Grant/WireImage for Think PR; p. 16 Frazer Harrison/Getty Images; pp. 19, 20 Gregg DeGuire/WireImage.

Library of Congress Cataloging-in-Publication Data

Rawson, Katherine.
  Brenda Song / Katherine Rawson.
      p. cm. — (Kid stars!)
  Includes index.
  ISBN 978-1-4042-8136-3 (library binding) — ISBN 978-1-4358-3406-4 (pbk.) — ISBN 978-1-4358-3407-1 (6-pack)
  1. Song, Brenda, 1988– —Juvenile literature. 2. Actresses—United States—Biography—Juvenile literature. 3. Asian-American Actresses—United States—Biography—Juvenile literature. I. Title.
  PN2287.S635R39 2010
  791.4302'8092—dc22
  [B]
                                                 2009008673

Manufactured in the United States of America

Contents

Meet Brenda Song 5
A Child Model 6
Going to Los Angeles 9
In the Movies 10
Brenda's Big Break 13
A Big Success 14
Playing a Warrior 17
Another Talent 18
The Sky's the Limit 21
Fun Facts 22
Glossary 23
Index 24
Web Sites 24

Brenda has played some fun, strong characters. She has a lot of fans who love watching her.

Meet Brenda Song

Brenda Song is one of the most talented and **popular** young stars in Hollywood. People know her best as London Tipton, the rich girl on the Disney show *The Suite Life of Zack & Cody*. Brenda has also appeared on several other shows, and she has been in many movies, too.

Brenda started working when she was very young. She first worked as a **model** before she started acting. Now, kids everywhere know who she is, and she has many fans. Let's find out more about Brenda's family, her work, and the things this bright new star hopes to do next!

A Child Model

Brenda Song was born on March 27, 1988, near Sacramento, California. Her father is Hmong, a member of a group of people who live in Southeast Asia, and her mother is from Thailand. Brenda has two younger brothers, named Timmy and Nathan.

One day when Brenda was very young, she was at a shopping mall with her family. An **agent** from a modeling school noticed her and wanted Brenda to go to the school. Her mother and father agreed, and Brenda started modeling shortly after. She was just five years old when she began working! What Brenda wanted next, though, was to be on TV.

Brenda's career started with modeling. However, Brenda knew she wanted to do more. She wanted to start acting.

Since moving to Los Angeles, Brenda (back left) has appeared at many events there. Here she is seen at Kids Day 2005 in Hollywood, an area of Los Angeles.

Going to Los Angeles

Brenda's first acting job was in a pizza **commercial** for Little Caesar's Pizza. Brenda and her mother then moved to Los Angeles so Brenda could get more jobs there. Two years later, the rest of the family moved there, too.

Brenda quickly got roles, or parts, on TV shows and in movies. Her first TV appearance was on the show *Thunder Alley*. Brenda's first movie role was in *Requiem*, in 1995. She played a young girl named Fong in that movie. Brenda also got parts on several other shows and movies, such as *100 Deeds for Eddie McDowd* and *Leave It to Beaver*.

In the Movies

In 2000, when she was 12, Brenda was in the Disney movie *The Ultimate Christmas Present*. It was an important movie for her because she won a Young Artist **Award** for her acting in it. This award is given to talented actors and musicians under the age of 18.

Brenda did not stop there. She appeared on several Disney Channel shows, such as *That's So Raven* and *Phil of the Future*. In 2004, she starred in the Disney TV movie *Stuck in the Suburbs*. About 3.7 **million** people watched the movie the first night it was on TV. Kids were now discovering who Brenda was!

Brenda (back center) appeared in the 2002 movie *Like Mike* with Crispin Glover (seated). Brenda played the character Reg.

Brenda became good friends with her *Suite Life* castmates, Dylan (left) and Cole (right) Sprouse. She said they looked out for each other on and off the show's set.

Brenda's Big Break

Next, Brenda got her biggest role yet. In 2005, she started playing the character London Tipton on *The Suite Life of Zack & Cody*. The show became a huge success, and it helped make Brenda a big star.

The Suite Life of Zack & Cody is about two boys, Zack and Cody, who live in a **hotel**. Brenda's character, London Tipton, is the daughter of the hotel's owner. She is very rich and **spoiled**. London likes shopping and talking about herself. She can do anything she wants, but she does not always do smart things. Even though London is spoiled, she can be funny sometimes.

A Big Success

Acting in *The Suite Life* kept Brenda very busy, but she loved her job. She became close with the other actors on the show, and they felt like another family to her. Brenda and the other cast members were all surprised and very happy when they learned that the show was a big hit.

The Suite Life of Zack & Cody was one of the most popular shows on the Disney Channel in 2005 and 2006. The show had several award **nominations**. Brenda herself was even nominated for her role as London. Kids everywhere loved watching the show, and they loved Brenda.

Brenda and Ashley Tisdale (right), who plays Maddie on *The Suite Life*, had worked with each other before. They both appeared on the show *Bette* in 2001.

Shin Koyamada plays the character Shen in *Wendy Wu*. In the movie, Shen helps Wendy train and teaches her martial arts.

Playing a Warrior

Brenda took time off from *The Suite Life* to star in the 2006 TV movie *Wendy Wu: Homecoming Warrior*. Brenda plays Wendy Wu, a teen who finds out that she is meant to be a warrior. Wendy must save the world, but she is too busy shopping and trying to be popular.

Brenda got to use **martial arts** skills that she learned as a child, and she trained for over two weeks. Brenda's hard work paid off. Around 5.7 million people watched the movie its first night. Brenda traveled to other countries to talk about the movie. She also appeared on **magazine** covers.

Another Talent

While Brenda was busy acting, she was also busy singing. She and other actors from the Disney Channel formed the Disney Channel Circle of Stars. Brenda sang with the group on the song "A Dream Is a Wish Your Heart Makes" on the album *DisneyMania 4*. The album was a big hit.

Brenda also recorded a song called "I'm Not That Girl" for *Wendy Wu: Homecoming Warrior*. She has also sung a number of times on *The Suite Life of Zack & Cody*. Some of her songs have been used in commercials on TV. We can hear Brenda's voice almost everywhere!

Brenda loves singing and says it is a lot of fun. When asked if she plans to sing in the future, she has said, "Never say never."

Brenda is thankful for her fans and for what has happened to her. As for what she will do next, Brenda says that whatever life brings her, she will do what is best!

The Sky's the Limit

In 2008, *The Suite Life of Zack & Cody* ended, but Brenda continued playing London Tipton on a new show called *The Suite Life on Deck*. Brenda also plays Nancy in the movie *College Road Trip*.

TV Guide named Brenda one of the "13 Hottest Young Stars to Watch" in 2008. Many of her fans agree with that, and they look forward to each new role she plays. What will Brenda do next? She plans to keep on acting. She looks forward to getting better as an actor and making her fans happy. As Brenda says, "The sky's the limit. Reach for the stars."

BRENDA SONG

 Brenda practices the martial art Tae Kwan Do, and she has earned a black belt in the sport.

 English was Brenda's **favorite** subject in school.

 She finished high school at age 16.

 She loves to bake.

 Brenda loves to eat Mexican food.

 Brenda's favorite basketball team is the Los Angeles Lakers.

 Her dog's name is Teddy.

 When she has some time off, Brenda enjoys shopping for shoes.

 Brenda is best friends with her *Suite Life* cast mate Ashley Tisdale.

 Brenda says that her role model is her mother.

Glossary

agent (AY-jent) A person who helps a model or actor with his or her job.

award (uh-WORD) A special honor given to someone.

commercial (kuh-MER-shul) A TV message trying to sell something.

favorite (FAY-vuh-rut) Most liked.

hotel (hoh-TEL) A place where you pay to stay overnight.

magazine (MA-guh-zeen) A weekly or monthly grouping of pictures and articles.

martial arts (MAR-shul ARTS) Types of self-defense or fighting that are practiced as sports.

million (MIL-yun) One thousand thousands.

model (MAH-dul) Someone who wears clothing in order to show what the clothing looks like.

nominations (nah-muh-NAY-shunz) Suggestions that someone or something should be given awards.

popular (PAH-pyuh-lur) Liked by lots of people.

spoiled (SPOY-uld) Someone who gets his or her own way too often.

warrior (WAR-yur) A person who fights in battles.

Index

A
album, 18

F
family, 5–6, 9, 14

L
Leave It to Beaver, 9

M
magazine, 17

modeling school, 6

R
role(s), 9, 13–14

S
Southeast Asia, 6
Suite Life of Zack & Cody, The, 13–14, 17–18, 21–22

T
teen, 17
That's So Raven, 10
Thunder Alley, 9
TV, 6, 9–10, 17–18, 21

W
warrior, 17
world, 17

Web Sites

Due to the changing nature of Internet links, PowerKids Press has developed an online list of Web sites related to the subject of this book. This site is updated regularly. Please use this link to access the list:
www.powerkidslinks.com/kids/song/